CANAAN,
NOW WHAT?

EDNA R. BARNETT

Copyright © 2015 by Edna R. Barnett

Canaan, Now What?
by Edna R. Barnett

Printed in the United States of America.
Edited by Xulon Press

ISBN 9781498438827

All rights reserved solely by the author. The author guarantees all contents are original and do not infringe upon the legal rights of any other person or work. No part of this book may be reproduced in any form without the permission of the author. The views expressed in this book are not necessarily those of the publisher.

Scripture quotations taken from the King James Version (KJV) – public domain

www.xulonpress.com

TABLE OF CONTENTS

Preface vii
Introduction... xi

God's Purpose for man's existence in the earth 17
Man in a Favorable Environment 18
Man Tested 19
The Result 21
The Universal Need 23
The Plan 25
The Process..28
The Exodus 31
Canaan ...A Journey ... Not a Destination..................36
Canaan 38
Now What?..39

PREFACE

Today it appears little is being said about the land of Canaan. Even when it is mentioned, it is usually referred to as simply, "The Promised Land." Admittedly, Canaan was indeed, The Promised Land; it was the land God promised to give to Abram *"and his descendants for an everlasting possession"* (Gen. 17:8, KJV). That Canaan was divinely designated for a perpetual ownership and, by a specific people, is an indication it was much more than just an ordinary geographic location.

From the beginning of creation, the plan of God is for mankind to consistently occupy a position of dominance in the earth. While historically, Canaan was a physical place located in the region of Palestine, between the Jordan River and the Mediterranean, symbolically it represented a territory in the earth which God initially had given to mankind from which to subdue, to replenish and to have dominion over the earth (See Gen. 1:28). Essentially, Canaan was distinctively, a specifically prepared place which God promised to a specifically prepared people for a specific divine purpose.

Thus, decisively as well as progressively Canaan became a place that God appointed for "a redeemed people". It was a place where the "redeemed people" would live as "the redeemed," and from that place, worship and serve their Redeemer.

Overall, Canaan was the physical preamble to God's comprehensive redemptive plan: the plan He established from before the foundations of the earth and of which He declared in the Garden of Eden following man's sin through disobedience and his subsequent fall. *"…the Lord God said unto the serpent, because thou hast done this, I will put enmity between thee and woman, and between thy seed and her seed; it shall bruise thy head, and thou shall bruise his heel*" (*Gen. 3:14-15*).

It was precisely that plan God had in mind when He approached a man named Abram, whose name would later be changed to Abraham and from whom "the Children of Israel" would come and instructed him to *leave* the place where he was living and to go to a place He would *show* him. That place was Canaan (Gen. 12:1; 17:3-8).

Because God is a God of plan and purpose, His instructions to Abram to leave his familiar surroundings and go to a place he did not know had to do with more than a simple, immediate, individual, geographic relocation. His promise to "*give to Abram and his descendants all the land of Canaan for an everlasting possession*" was more than just the promise of a real estate endowment. The instruction along with the promise ultimately had to do with an imminent transposition of people—a move that would not only transfer "a people" out of natural bondage and into natural freedom, but it would also signal the opportunity for a universal spiritual relocation; a move that would ultimately provide deliverance from a life of spiritual bondage to a life of spiritual freedom.

Hence, the physical land of Canaan which God had appointed and promised to Abram and to all his descendants for an everlasting possession was a symbol of a spiritual Canaan ... a position or place which God expects all of His people to come into, and from that place or position live as the freed.

Jesus Christ's coming into the world—the world where all its inhabitants were—"*all their lifetime subject to bondage*" was the initial step toward the fulfillment of that plan. Luke 1:43 states: "Blessed be the Lord God of Israel; for He hath visited and redeemed His people." Christ's coming into the world as "Savior" was the supreme means for a universal spiritual relocation, a removal of all mankind from the "kingdom of darkness" into the "kingdom of light."

That the physical land of Canaan typified a spiritual one; assuredly, Jesus Christ, "The Redeemer", coming into the world and redeeming mankind from the bondage of sin subsequently makes spiritual Canaan a promised inheritance to be obtained by all who choose to receive Jesus Christ as Savior and Lord.

It is God's desire to have all of mankind saved and come into the knowledge of the truth. While many people are saved (have "received" Jesus), many, however, have not progressed onto knowing the magnitude of their possession. They are ignorant of the fact that being saved brings them into a relationship with God, which makes them heirs of an inheritance—an inheritance that includes forgiveness of sin and deliverance from the dominion of it. As a result of this ignorance, many live in fear, misery, and defeat. They live as if still in bondage and governed by sin. To be forgiven of sin, and delivered from the dominion of it, and yet live as though still in bondage is an absolute denial of the delivering, sustaining power of God.

It is the realization of this truth that has moved me to write *Canaan, Now What?* to primarily point out not only the benefits that come as a result of inheriting Canaan, but also the responsibilities associated with possessing it.

INTRODUCTION

From an early age I became pretty familiar with many of the stories in the Bible, particularly the ones in the Old Testament, such as: David, a youth, slaying the ungodly giant Goliath (1 Sam. 17:22-54); of three Hebrew boys, though in Babylonian captivity, refused to violate their godly resolves, and as a result were thrown in a fiery furnace (Dan. 3). Also of Daniel, a prominent assistant to a Babylonian King, thrown into a den of lions because of his decision to pray only to the God of heaven (Dan. 6:1-17). Of Joseph, a young adult, incarcerated in Egypt's prison because of sibling rivalry (Gen. 37:2-36). Also of the exodus of the children of Israel—Abraham's descendants out of four hundred years of bondage in the land of Egypt and their entry into The Promised Land of Canaan (Ex. 12:31-51).

Hearing Bible stories was not an unusual custom for most children when I was growing up. Bible stories were often taught in the church, in the homes, and also in the schools. I must say, as a child I had no understanding of the meaning or purpose of them, or why it was (seemingly) mandatory they be widely taught. What I did have, however, was a solid belief all the stories were true. I totally believed everything written in those stories actually happened.

I have heard it said the "things we learn in life never disappear." Over time, I came to realize those stories have been indelibly etched in the walls of my mind. They undoubtedly "seeded" my heart and my mind with an enduring measure of hopefulness and certainly have been a vital element in the foundation of my faith in God.

I accepted Jesus Christ as my Saviour when I was ten years old. One Sunday afternoon, on my way home from Sunday school, which was a three-mile walk I often did alone, I decided to challenge myself by memorizing the scripture verses of the text which was given in Sunday school that day. The text was John 1:1-13:

> *In the beginning was the Word, and the Word was with God, and the Word was God. The same was in the beginning with God. All things were made by Him; and without Him was not any thing made that was made, in Him was life; and the life was the light of men. And the light shineth in darkness; and the darkness comprehended it not. There was a man sent from God, whose name was John. The same came for a witness, to bear witness of the Light that all men through Him might believe. He was not that Light, but was sent to bear witness of that Light. That was the true Light, which lighteth every man that cometh into the world. He was in the world, and the world was made by Him and the world knew Him not. He came unto His own, and His own received Him not. But as many as received Him, to them gave He power to become the sons of God, even to them that believe on His name; which were born, not of blood, nor of the will of the flesh, nor of the will of man, but of God.*

Although I had memorized all thirteen verses, verse twelve vividly stood out in my mind: *"But as many as received Him, to them gave He power to become the sons of God, even to them that believe on His name."* Admittedly, I did not understand the full meaning of the verse. However, like I did with the Bible stories, I believed the words and repeated them several times during the week that followed.

On the following Sunday night, my mother—who was already saved—and I attended a revival service at a church where the building was still under construction. I vividly recall going into the building and walking in sawdust to find a seat on one of the wooden folding chairs because neither the floors nor the pews were installed.

Introduction

Little of what the preacher said that night made any sense to me. In fact, I cannot even recall what the title of his message was. However, as was expected of me and all the other children who were there, I listened. At the end of the message, the preacher asked if there was anyone who would like to accept Jesus Christ as Savior to raise his or her hand and come to the altar for prayer. Even without understanding much of what was preached, I immediately stood up and walked bravely to the altar with a few others. The preacher thanked us for coming forward, prayed for us, and then told us we were saved. We returned to our seats and waited for the service to dismiss. All the while, my mother just sat quietly nodding her head and smiling.

On the way home neither my mother nor I said a word to each other. However, as soon as we got home and into the house, my mother looked at me in the eye and uttered these unforgettable words: "Well Edna you are a saved girl now!"

As far as I was concerned though, going to the altar, being prayed for, and hearing I was now saved only added to my lack of understanding of spiritual things. I did not understand what being saved really meant. Nor did I know how to explain to anyone what exactly happened to me on that Sunday night when I raised my hand to say, "Yes, I want to accept Jesus Christ as my Savior," and then went up to the altar for prayer.

Despite my limited understanding of what being "saved" really meant, and although I could hardly explain my "altar experience" (especially since physically nothing about me had changed, nor did I exhibit any emotional response), one thing was absolutely clear to me: between memorizing John 1:1-13 and my saying "Yes, I want to receive Jesus Christ as my Savior", "something" indescribable happened in my heart. And as a result of that "something", I would be able to go to heaven instead of going to hell when I die.

At that time, the church I was regularly attending was a missions-oriented one. To me that meant as soon as someone got saved, they were encouraged to consider becoming missionaries so they could be "exported" to the "mission field." I say "exported" because to me it appeared the "mission field" was only in foreign countries. Apparently, the missionaries who came to the church were all from foreign countries, and the ones who were sent from the church all went into foreign countries. However, as I got older, I began to silently question why the "mission field" could not also be the home, the workplace, the school, and the community at large, instead of it only being in foreign lands.

Since at that time apparently that was the rule, as time went on, I convinced myself that the reason the mission field is in foreign countries is that the stories in the Bible all took place in foreign lands. So the "mission field" most likely has to also be in foreign lands.

That thinking led me to also begin questioning the relevancy of the Bible stories in present-day ordinary living. For a while, I started thinking the stories were mostly about ancient people who lived in faraway places and had experienced strange and unusual circumstances. I thought they had nothing to do with ordinary people (especially of my day) or with normal day-to-day issues or situations, and definitely nothing to do with being saved.

Furthermore, in the island of Jamaica, which is where I was living, there were no lions that I could ever imagine being locked up with as Daniel was. I only knew the domestic animals such as the cows, donkeys, pigs, goats, and chickens. I also did not know of any "fiery furnaces." The only thing that even came close to being a fiery furnace like the one in which the three Hebrew boys were thrown was the heat of the island's sun, or the heat from the open flames of the firestand from which we cooked our food. And the thought of ever confronting a real giant like David did was unimaginable. To me the only giant any child or I would ever face are our parents (or any adult for that matter) whom we would dare to disobey or disrespect. The likelihood of that ever happening was rare since none of us was that insane.

The idea of the "mission field" being only in foreign countries was not the only thing I secretly wondered about. I also had questions like: now that I am saved, what's next? Or, what does it mean to live like a "saved person"?

No one appeared to have answers to these questions. In retrospect, no one could. Over time, I came to understand those were not just simple questions in the mind of a child. I later realized those were divine inquiries—inquiries to which the answers are divinely and progressively revealed. In fact, I later realized it is precisely what Jesus was implying when He said to His disciples, *"I have many things to say to you, but ye cannot bear them now. Howbeit, when He, the Spirit of Truth is come, He will guide you into all truth"* (John 16:12-13). Gradually I began to understand receiving Jesus Christ as Savior is only the initial step to being "born again"; that subsequent to the "new birth" are developmental steps, which are vitally essential for the personal and spiritual growth and maturity of the believer.

GOD'S PURPOSE FOR MAN'S EXISTENCE IN THE EARTH

W hen God said, *"Let us make man in our own image, after our likeness; and let them have dominion over the fish of the sea, and over the fowl of the air, and over the cattle, and over all the earth, and over every creeping thing that creepeth upon the earth"* (Gen. 1:26), His intent was to bring into being a species of creation that would not only reflect Godliness in the earth, but would also be responsible for governing the earth.

With that in mind, *"God created man in His own image ... male and female He created them."* He created man a triune being. This means man was created a spirit being, having a soul and living in a body. *"...And God blessed them..."* Then He instructed them concerning His purpose for their existence in the earth (Gen. 1:27).

Essentially, God purposefully created man and equipped him with the means to fulfill the purpose. He created man with the ability to communicate with God, to have control of his behavior, and to exercise dominion over his environment.

MAN IN A FAVORABLE ENVIRONMENT

From the beginning of creation God is seen as provider, consistently meeting the needs of His creation. Not only did God endow man with the ability to demonstrate godly characteristics on the earth, He also provided the means to meet man's emotional needs. Then He put man in an environment that had the potential to produce everything necessary to meet his physical needs. Thus giving man the freedom to do what he was created to do, which is to reflect godliness on the earth and to govern his environment.

> *And the Lord God said, "it is not good that the man should be alone; I will make him a help meet for him." And the Lord God caused a deep sleep to fall upon Adam ... and He took one of his ribs, and closed up the flesh thereof; and the rib, which the Lord God had taken from the man, made He a woman, and brought her unto the man. And the Lord God planted a garden eastward in Eden; and there He put the man whom He had formed ... And God said, "behold, I have given you every herb bearing seed which is upon the face of all the earth, and every tree, in the which, is the fruit of a tree yielding seed: to you it shall be for meat."* (Gen. 2:8; 2:18, 21-22; 1:29)

MAN TESTED...

By divine design, authority inevitably carries with it the challenge of stewardship responsibility. In addition to having the right to govern the earth, man was also responsible for guarding his surroundings.

> *The Lord God took the man, and put him into the Garden of Eden to dress it and to keep it, and the Lord God commanded the man, saying of every tree of the garden thou mayest freely eat: but of the tree of the knowledge of good and evil, thou shalt not eat of it: for in the day that thou eatest thereof thou shalt surely die (Gen. 2:16-17).*

1 Cor. 4:2 states "...it is required in stewards, that a man be found faithful." In the natural employers usually make their hiring decisions based on the noticeable potential of the prospective employee to meet the organization's objective. However, along with having potential to do the work, employers also expect the employee to exhibit an inclination to not only comply with the organization's rules and regulations, but to also protect its "brand".

That God appointed man to be caretaker of the garden clearly indicates man had the potential to do the job. However, to "dress" the garden and "to keep it" required more than potential. It required man's willingness to comply with the instruction God had given. Basically, the divine, delegated authority required man to not only exercise his God-given influence in the earth, but also to make a decision to choose to obey God. For man to do that, it was necessary for him to be tested. The result of which would reveal not only man's willingness or unwillingness to obey God, but it would also prove whether or not he could be trusted with the life-long responsibility of reflecting godliness in the earth and of governing his environment.

God's command to man "not eat of the tree of the knowledge of good and evil" was not to impose any dietary restrictions, nor was it intended to deprive man of any of the provisions He had made for him in the garden. The prohibition was to primarily test man's willingness to obey God. Additionally, it was to protect man from the subtle intrusion of evil and to expose the demising deceitfulness of Satan.

> *Now the serpent was more subtil than any beast of the field which the Lord God had made. And he said unto the woman, "yea, hath God said, 'ye shall not eat of every tree of the garden'?" And the woman said unto the serpent, "we may eat of the fruit of the trees of the garden: but of the fruit of the tree which is in the midst of the garden, God hath said, 'ye shall not eat of it, neither shall ye touch it, lest ye die.'" And the serpent said unto the woman, "ye shall not surely die: for God doth know that in the day ye eat thereof, then your eyes shall be opened, and ye shall be as gods, knowing good and evil." When the woman saw that the tree was good for food, and that it was pleasant to the eyes, and a tree to be desired to make one wise, she took of the fruit thereof, and did eat, and gave also unto her husband with her; and he did eat"* (Gen. 3:1-6).

THE RESULT…

As in normal employment situations when an employee having the potential and the wherewithal to accomplish what the employer expects and being made aware of what behaviors are acceptable or unacceptable, yet refuses to comply or perform as expected, is clearly a demonstration of intentional rebellion. A behavior which, if left unaddressed, has the potential to not only pollute the morale of the organization, but to also set the stage for the ruin of it. Handling unacceptable behavior is vital to the overall success of any organization. Often it requires disciplinary actions such as suspension without pay, and/or termination of employment.

In the same way with spiritual matters, man having the divine ability to guard his surroundings, and knowing what God expects of him, yet chose to "eat of the tree of the knowledge of good and evil" was a conscious and deliberate act of disobedience to God, a display of utter rebellion against Him. A rebellion that had the potential to not only cause man's demise, but also ruin his environment.

That initial act of disobedience to God was the gateway through which sin entered into man and entirely contaminated him. It corrupted his nature, it polluted his conscience, it darkened his understanding, and it caused his thoughts and his affections to become sensual and evil (Rom. 1:21; Eph. 4:18). So destructive was that act of disobedience, it not only debased man, but it also initiated a severing of the relationship between man and God—a relationship God intended to be eternally intact.

The condition left man at a complete loss. Man lost protection from disease and from sorrow. He lost protection from hardships and from sufferings and he lost access to the tree of life. Man essentially became depraved and deprived—a condition that rendered him totally incapable of governing his environment. So similar to natural employment situations where the employer immediately addresses the unacceptable employee's behavior; in the same way God immediately dealt with the issue of man's disobedience. He suspended man from his position as caretaker of the Garden. *"…the Lord God sent him forth from the Garden of Eden… So he drove out the man; and he placed at the east of the Garden of Eden Cherubims…"* (Gen. 3:23–24).

THE UNIVERSAL NEED...

Man's disobedience to God's command not only bereft him of his God-given position, but it also robbed him of his God-given possession. Alienated from God, man was now susceptible to evil and its imminent effects. Man became "the ruled" instead of being "the ruler." He became the slave instead of being the master. *"...for of whom a man is overcome, of the same is he brought into bondage"* (2 Peter 2:19). Essentially, man's disobedience to God gave to Satan the means to become "the god of this world", thus putting man in a position to become the slave to Satan. *"To whom ye yield yourselves servants to obey, his servants ye are to whom ye obey; whether of sin unto death, or of obedience unto righteousness"* (Rom. 6:16).

Adam's sin through disobedience ultimately initiated the ruin of humanity. It set in motion a progressive deterioration in the heart and in the mind of mankind, a condition that subsequently generated a devastating, burdensome, long-term effect on all of creation.

> *Unto the woman He said, "I will greatly multiply thy sorrow and thy conception; in sorrow thou shalt bring forth children; and thy desire shall be to thy husband, and he shall rule over thee." And unto Adam he said, "because thou hast hearkened unto the voice of thy wife, and has eaten of the tree of which I commanded thee saying, thou shalt not eat of it ... cursed is the ground for thy sake; in sorrow shalt thou eat of it all the days of thy life; thorns also and thistles shall it*

bring forth to thee; and thou shalt eat the herb of the field; in the sweat of thy face shalt thou eat bread..." (Gen. 3:16-19)

"...Adam lived an hundred and thirty years, and begat a son in his own likeness, after his image..." (Gen. 5:3).

The impact of Adam's sin, through disobedience, undoubtedly had an enduring universal effect on not just humanity, but on all of creation. "...as *by one man sin entered into the world, and death by sin; and so death passed upon all men..." (*Rom. 5:12). Everyone born subsequent to Adam inevitably inherits not only the nature of Adam, the propensity to sin, but also the consequences of his sin. Consequences that include sickness, disease, sorrow, fear, poverty, anger, and death—a condition God never intended for mankind. Man's inevitable predicament was by no means a surprise to God. Long before Adam sinned, God knew he would and that as a result of it, all of creation would suffer, all of humanity would plunge into bondage, a state God never intended for mankind, thus creating the need for a divine universal deliverance.

THE PLAN...

Even though man, through his own volition, was spiritually dislocated from God and confined to the captivity of Satan, the love God has for mankind did not change. II Sam. 14:14 states: *"For we must needs die, and are as water spilt on the ground, which cannot be gathered up again; neither doth God respect any person: yet doth he devise means, that His banished be not expelled from Him."* So the ensuing dilemma did not, in any way, cancel or alter God's plan and purpose for mankind. Instead, it revealed the immeasurable degree of love God has for mankind along with His eternal commitment to not only pursue a relationship with mankind, but to also preserve that relationship. In fact so committed is God to the success and the prosperity of mankind, that from the foundation of the world, He had in place a universal rescue plan; a plan that would not only liberate mankind from the servitude of Satan, but it would also provide the means by which man could be restored to a relationship with God and reendowed with the capacity to not only govern his environment, but also to demonstrate godliness in the earth.

Steps toward the unveiling of the rescue plan became evident when God approached a man named Abram, whose name was later changed to Abraham (Gen. 17:5) and instructed him to leave the place he was living and to go to a place He would show him. Ultimately, the overall plan of God is to produce a new species of people, a people that would be willing to trust Him and obey Him, and with whom He would have continual fellowship.

Abram proved to be the channel God could use to bring into existence such a people, and through whom He could illustrate His rescue plan for mankind. When God said to Abram, *"Get thee out of thy country, and from thy kindred, and from thy father's house, unto a land that I will shew thee"* (Gen. 12:1), Abram believed God and he obeyed God. Implying Canaan was divinely designated for a perpetual ownership and by a specific people, God also said to Abram, *" I will give unto thee, and to thy seed after thee, the land wherein thou art a stranger, all the land of Canaan, for an everlasting possession; and I will be their God"* (Gen. 17:8).

Invariably, every command or instruction God gives to man, He supports with a promise. Fulfillment of the promise most often requires man's obedience to what God says. Obedience to God's command, even when it does not make sense, is vital to obtaining the promises of God. So similar to instructing Adam and expecting him to obey, God instructed Abram expecting him to also obey.

Unlike Adam, Abram obeyed God. Without resisting, and without knowing where he was going, Abram, in obedience to God, left the comfort and the familiarities of where he was living and trusted God to take Him to a place he did not know (Heb. 11:8). So essential was Abram's obedience to God; it "was credited to him as righteousness" (Gen. 15:6). Abram's willingness to trust God and to obey Him moved God to choose him and his descendants, the children of Israel (as they were later called), to "show" to the entire world what He would do for any people who would likewise trust Him and obey Him.

Along with the instruction to leave the security of his surroundings, and the promise to give to him and his descendants *"all the land of Canaan, for an everlasting possession"* was also the warning of an impending captivity that the Children of Israel (Abraham's offspring) would experience. With that though, God assured Abram of their deliverance out of it. He said to Abram, *"Know of a surety that thy seed shall be a stranger in a land that is not theirs, and shall serve them; and they shall afflict them four hundred years; and also that nation, whom they shall serve, will I judge: and afterward shall they come out with great substance"* (Gen. 15:13-14).

Between Abram obeying God's command to leave the place he was living and the fulfillment of God's promise to *"bless him, and to make of him a great nation, and to make his name great"*, a number of significant providential events occurred—all of which were divinely connected to the promise of Canaan. Events such as God changing Abram's name to Abraham, signifying He had made him "a father of many nations" (Gen. 17:5). Following that, Abraham at the age of ninety-nine produced a son – as God had promised he would (Gen. 17:19; 18:14; 21:1-3)—then later, required of him to offer that son for a burnt offering (Gen. 22:2).

Because God's plan for mankind is a "plan to prosper, not to harm; a plan to give hope and a future" (Jer. 29:11), whenever He requires something of man that appears to be sacrificial, as with the command to Adam not to eat of *"the tree of the knowledge of good and evil,"* the intent is never to impose hardship. Nor is it to deprive man of the blessings God has given. The requirement, though seemingly sacrificial, most often is to increase the blessings. What God expects, however, is a willingness of man to surrender the blessings to Him if and when He requires it. For example, when He required of Abraham to offer his only son for a burnt offering. Abraham, without hesitation and without question, obediently prepared himself, prepared the altar for the burnt offering, and willing proceeded to offer his only son for a burnt offering (Gen. 22:3-10).

It is consistently evident God never requires, or expects anything of His creation for which He does not make provision for the fulfillment of it. God is Creator, He is Protector, and He is Provider– He provides resources, and He provides opportunities. Prov. 14:26 states, "In the fear of the Lord is strong confidence and his children shall have a place of refuge." As soon as Abraham began to sacrifice his only son, God intercepted his actions and commanded him not to do anything to his son, saying to him, *"now I know that thou fearest God, seeing thou has not withheld thy son, thine only son from me"* (Gen. 22:12).

Not only did God recognize and commend Abraham for his reverence and obedience to Him, but He also rewarded him for his willingness to offer his only son for a burnt offering. God immediately provided a ram for Abraham to offer as the burnt offering instead of offering his son (Gen. 22:13).

THE PROCESS...

Following Abram's test of faith and obedience was the fulfillment of a number of promises God had made to him. Such as the increase of Abraham's seed – the Children of Israel, the migrating of them to the land of Egypt, the establishing of them as a nation (Gen. 35:10-11), and as God had forewarned Abraham, the onset of their enslavement in the land of Egypt. God is sovereign. His plan and purpose are eternal. He determines the timeframes and the methods to accomplish it.

The Children of Israel's trip to the land of Egypt turned into four hundred years of Egyptian servitude. Under the rulership of Pharaoh, *"the Egyptians made the children of Israel to serve with rigor; and they made their lives bitter with hard bondage"* (Ex. 1:13–14). God's way of working has to do with His overall plan and purpose for mankind. He is not influenced by time, by situations, or by circumstances. So the severe oppression along with the apparent hopelessness the Children of Israel were undergoing while in Egypt did not in any way hinder His plan. Instead, it emphasized the divine providence and sovereignty. In fact, everything the Children of Israel experienced pointed to the divine universal deliverance plan (See Gen. 15:13-14). As a matter of fact, over and over, God reminded them of who He is and His plan to establish them there in Egypt. Time after time, He assured them of His commitment to be with them there, and to bring them out again. *"I am God, the God of thy father: fear not to go down into Egypt: for I will there make of thee a great nation. I will go down with thee into Egypt and I will surely bring thee up again"* (Gen. 46:3-4, 47:27).

While God's method of executing His plan may be unpredictable, the accomplishing of it is always sure. What is also consistently evident is that from the beginning of creation God's plan is to partner with mankind–to give mankind the opportunity to "co-labor" with Him. The fulfillment of God's promise to the Children of Israel to *"surely bring them up again"* began when God, through a burning bush which was not consumed appeared to a man whose name was Moses, and said to him:

> *I am the God of thy father, the God of Abraham, the God of Isaac, and the God of Jacob...I have surely seen the affliction of my people which are in Egypt, and have heard their cry by reason of their taskmasters; for I know their sorrows; and I am come down to deliver them out of the hand of the Egyptians, and to bring them up out of that land unto a good land and a large, unto a land flowing with milk and honey; unto the place of the Canaanites. Come now therefore, and I will send thee unto Pharaoh, that thou mayest bring forth my people the children of Israel out of Egypt.* (Ex. 3: 6-10)

It has been said, "service is the rent you pay for the space you occupy on earth." This certainly holds true regarding the Children of Israel. During their time in Egypt, *"the Egyptians made them to serve with rigor"* (Ex. 1:13-14), but the function of serving did not originate with the Egyptians. It originated with God. According to Gen. 2:8, it was introduced when *"the Lord God planted a garden eastward in Eden; and there He put man whom He had formed ... and the Lord God took the man, and put him into the Garden of Eden to dress it and to keep it."* So God's idea of serving is distinctly different from that of the Egyptians—they "made the children of Israel to serve with rigor."

Primarily, serving is a function God established to be a benefit and privilege to mankind and not a burden. It provides an opportunity for man to partner with God in matters concerning the livelihood of all of mankind. Which is why God, at the outset of disclosing His plan to deliver the Children of Israel out of Egypt's bondage, and to bring them into the Promised Land (Canaan), He emphasized to Moses when the Israelites are brought out of the land of Egypt, they would serve Him at the appointed place (Ex. 3:12). His intent was that they do so without fear (Luke 1:74-75). Essentially, service is an expression of gratitude for the provision of freedom. It is precisely why God commissioned Moses to say to Pharaoh, *"Israel is my son, even my firstborn: And I say unto thee, 'Let my son go, that he may serve me'"* (Ex. 4:22-23).

God knows everything about everything. Yet sovereignly, He does not always explain every detail concerning the outcome of His directives. Since His "thoughts are not like our thoughts; neither are our ways like His ways," following His directions is no guarantee there may not be challenges or disappointments. In fact quite often, it is in the midst of obeying God that oppositions, obstacles, and disappointments often arise. For example, when Moses accepted the assignment to go tell Pharaoh to release the Children of Israel that they may serve their God, he was definitely following God's directives. However, to Moses' surprise, when he confronted Pharaoh with the request, things did not go the way he expected them to go. Instead Pharaoh's heart became hardened and he made the lives of the Israelites even more burdensome.

Pharaoh's unyielding refusal to let the Israelites go was no doubt frustrating and understandably discouraging to Moses. God, however, was not moved by Pharaoh's stubbornness or Moses' emotions. Instead, He repeatedly affirmed Himself to Moses and assured him of His commitment to redeem the Children of Israel out of the Egyptian bondage. He said:

> *I am the Lord, and I will bring you out from under the burdens of the Egyptians, and I will rid you out of their bondage, and I will redeem you with a stretched out arm and with great judgments: and I will take you to me for a people, and I will be to you a God: and ye shall know that I am the Lord your God which bringeth you out from under the burdens of the Egyptians. And I will bring you in unto the land, concerning the which I did swear to give it to Abraham, to Isaac, and to Jacob; and I will give it you for an heritage: I am the Lord.* (Ex. 6:6-8)

THE EXODUS...

When Adam failed the test of obedience in the Garden of Eden and was subsequently dismissed from there, God did not abandon His expectation of mankind: there will always be a people in the earth who will serve Him and obey His commands. In fact, to affirm that expectation, God, in the midst of declaring to Adam the consequences of his disobedience, also decreed a plan in which the process would inevitably involve a Redeemer (Gen. 3:15), a Redeemer who would be capable of producing such a people. So then, when He directed Moses to say to Pharaoh, *"Israel is my son, even my firstborn: And I say unto thee, 'Let my son go, that he may serve me,'"* not only was He announcing subsequent to Israel there would be other "sons", but He was also indicating that like Israel, they would also be expected to serve Him.

Basically, while Israel's servitude in Egypt was a physical one and specific to them, its overall significance had to do with a universal spiritual captivity. It represented the spiritual bondage to which all of mankind was subject, and which all of mankind inherited as a result of Adam's sin through his disobedience to God. Hence, Israel's exodus out of Egypt was by no means just an ordinary migration. Their leaving Egypt was a divinely ordained evacuation which was a symbol of a forthcoming universal spiritual deliverance – a deliverance that would ultimately free mankind from the bondage of sin to position of total liberty.

The fact that God does not change is consistently evident in all of His dealings with mankind. While His methods may vary, His overall plan and purpose for mankind remain steadfast; which plan and purpose is that mankind not only reflect "Godlikeness" in the earth, but also have dominion over it (Gen. 1:26, Psalm 8:5-8).

In keeping that plan and that purpose alive, beginning in the Garden of Eden, God consistently tested man's willingness to follow divine instructions. He tested Adam when He commanded him to not eat "of the tree of the knowledge of good and evil" (Gen. 2:17); He tested Abram when He instructed him to leave the place he was living and to go to a place He would show him (Gen. 12:1); and He tested the children of Israel to "prove" whether or not they would keep His commandments. (See Ex. 16:4; Deut. 8:2:16).

By contrast, Israel's coming out of Egypt and their journeying into the land of Canaan can be compared to the physical birth and development process. For example, with physical birth, the labor period sometimes takes hours and is usually quite painful. However, once labor is over, birth generally follows, and often pretty quickly. Following birth is the progression to childhood then onto becoming a mature, responsible adult, a process that usually takes years – for some at least twenty-one years. Between the stages of birth and childhood, instinctively the child relies on the parents to provide the basic needs such as food, shelter, and clothing. However, in addition to meeting those basic needs, it is vitally important that the child be nurtured, disciplined, and instructed.

Although the majority of Israelites who came out of Egypt were adults physically, collectively, they all were spiritually like newborn babies. They were God's "firstborn". Similar to the physical birth process, their time of "labor" in Egypt was long and difficult. Leaving though, was relatively quick: *they departed with haste.*

As with physical "newborns", the Israelites, being spiritual "newborns", also needed to be provided for. They needed to be nurtured. They needed to be disciplined and they needed to be instructed. God, their Heavenly Father, had committed to doing that. In fact, He assured them saying:

> *I will take you to me for a people, and I will be to you*
> *a God: and ye shall know that I am the Lord your God*
> *which bringeth you out from under the burdens of the*

Egyptians. And I will bring you in unto the land, concerning the which I did swear to give it to Abraham, to Isaac, and to Jacob; and I will give it you for an heritage: I am the Lord" (Ex. 6:6 -8).

Just as natural children are expected to develop and progress from infancy into adulthood, in the same way God expected Israel–His "Firstborn"—to grow from spiritual infancy into spiritual adulthood. Also, as with physical development, spiritual development is a process that usually takes time. For the children of Israel, that time was significantly long.

Between Egypt and Canaan was *the land of the Philistines*, which geographically, was a direct route between both lands. However, God did not allow the Children of Israel to take the direct route. Instead, He led them through *"the way of the wilderness"*, a wide stretch of land. *"And it came to pass, when Pharaoh had let the people go, that God led them not through the way of the land of the Philistines, although that was near…but God led the people about, through the way of the wilderness of the Red Sea"* (Ex. 13:17-18).

This wilderness way, although a farther route into Canaan, was not intended to be punitive to the Children of Israel. The extended way was to provide the time and the place to rid themselves of their Egyptian appetites and tendencies, to abandon their servitude mentality, and adopt the mindset of freedom. Essentially, "the way of the wilderness", though considerably long, was their divinely appointed institution for learning.

With most learning institutions, the general objective is the student progresses from the elementary level of learning to a level of proficiency and to eventually leave the institution as responsible, employable, and profitable people in the world. In the same way, God's overall expectation of the children of Israel was for them to learn, develop, and become responsible, disciplined people in their Promised Land: Canaan. "The way of the wilderness" was the route or the process He determined for them take in order to become "that people." It was by "the way of the wilderness" they were to learn to develop their trust in God and to rely on Him to meet all of their needs. It was where they were to learn the ways of God and the principles of God that are vitally essential for living victoriously in their Promised Land: Canaan.

Sadly though, the Children of Israel did not embrace God's expectation of them. Even though God had miraculously delivered them *"by his own hand"* out of Egypt's bondage, and assured them of His enduring provision and protection, obeying Him, and relying on Him to meet their every need was not something they were inclined to doing.

Soon after leaving Egypt and on their way to Canaan, rather than believing God, and obeying, and trusting Him, they began to complain and to murmur. *"The whole congregation of the children of Israel murmured against Moses and Aaron in the wilderness"* (Ex. 16:1- 3). As a result, instead of maturing to spiritual adulthood, they remained undisciplined, irresponsible babes. Subsequently, their development years were unusually many: forty extra years they wandered in the wilderness (Deut. 1:2). Not only did their rebellion and disobedience to God delay their entry into the land of Canaan, but it also prevented the majority of those who were delivered out of Egypt's bondage from entering (Num. 14:30-35; Heb. 3:10).

God is always present and actively at work. Because His promises are connected to His overall plan and purpose for mankind, the emphasis is not so much on what the Children of Israel did or did not do, but more on what God did. He delivered them out of the bondage of Egypt and brought them into a land of freedom as He said He would.

From the time man fell in the Garden of Eden because of his disobedience, to the time when Abraham moved from where he was living to the place God promised to "show" him was considerably long. Also long was the time between the Children of Israel's wanderings in the wilderness to the time of the arrival of the "few" who entered the land of Canaan. However, time, situations, or circumstances do not prevent or alter the execution of God's plan. If anything, it increases the certainty of it. Hence, whether it is forty years, or four hundred years, what God promises He fulfills. So in spite of the number of the Children of Israel who, because of their rebelliousness did not make it into the land of Canaan, and regardless of the seemingly long time between when God promised Abram to deliver his "seed" out of bondage, to the actual fulfillment of it, the performing of the promise was absolutely sure. Therefore, just as sure to be fulfilled was the promise God made to the serpent in the Garden, when he deceived the woman, which promise was that "the seed of the woman shall bruise his head".

CANAAN... A JOURNEY – NOT A DESTINATION

Though Canaan was undoubtedly the place God designated for the Children of Israel to live once they were delivered out of Egypt's bondage, it was not to be the end of their pilgrimage. Their arrival in the land was essentially the beginning of a "lifelong journey" as a redeemed people—a journey which gave them the opportunity to live out what they had been taught and hopefully learned during their wilderness wanderings. Overall, Canaan represented the manifested faithfulness of God in fulfilling His promise.

Understandably, after leaving Egypt's four hundred years of servitude, anything even remotely laborious was—to any of those Israelites who entered Canaan—something to be avoided. Nevertheless, to their surprise and perhaps disappointment, there was much work to be done in the land.

Even though they were living in *"goodly houses"* in a land filled with grapes and figs, and flowed with milk and honey (as God had promised), they were not exempt from the labor of it. Along with the abundant provisions in the land was a corresponding amount of work. Particularly the kind of work that is usually associated with such provisions as what the Children of Israel had come into. For example, the "goodly houses" had to be maintained, the vineyards had to be dressed, the figs and grapes had to be harvested, the cows had to be milked, and the honey had to be extracted from the honeycomb (while at the same time contending with the bees). Furthermore, the Canaanites, along with other nations whom had God said He would drive out, were still living in the land (Ex. 23:29-30). Which meant on a regular basis, the Children of Israel had to interact with a diverse group of people; people whom apparently did not know God, neither did they fear Him. As such did not accept their beliefs nor their way of living, but who, nonetheless, were included in God's redemptive plan.

In reality, Canaan was in no way "a bed of roses" for the Children of Israel. In fact, living there, they encountered all the day-to-day issues, which were "common" to mankind. However, it was there that they had the opportunity to (regardless of what was going on around them) illustrate the benefits of serving God. It was there they could be credible witnesses of the demonstrated faithfulness and power of God in delivering them, in protecting them, and in providing for them.

Basically, Canaan was the platform from which the Children of Israel were to model to the rest of the nations what God would do for any people who will believe Him, who will trust Him, and who will obey Him. *"He ... gave them the lands of the heathen: and they inherited the labor of the people: that they might observe his statutes, and keep his laws"* (Psalm 105:44-45).

On the whole, Israel's time in Egypt, combined with their wilderness experiences, and their living in the land of Canaan, were not at all coincidental. All of "it happened to them for examples." Altogether, it was the process God chose to demonstrate not only His sovereignty, but also His intent to bring them into a relationship with Him, of which providentially, is recorded as a warning to all subsequent believers (1 Cor. 10:11).

CANAAN...

When God initially blessed man and said to them, "replenish the earth, and subdue it and have dominion over..." (Gen. 1:28), the blessing was not limited to Adam, neither was the command exclusively theirs. The plan of God was the blessing, along with the command, be adopted and accomplished by all humanity subsequent to Adam.

However, when Adam sinned by disobeying God's command, there came into existence a universal spiritual bondage–a bondage to which all humanity subsequent to Adam was predictably subjected (Heb. 2:15). As a result, all succeeding humanity fell short of exercising their God-given authority. So, when God, in preparation for Israel's deliverance out of Egypt's bondage, commissioned Moses to say to Pharaoh, *"Israel is my son, even my firstborn: and I say unto thee, 'Let my son go, that he may serve me'"* (Exo 4:22-23), not only was He declaring to Pharaoh Israel's approaching deliverance, but He was also sending a message to all humanity, who although not in a physical bondage as the Children of Israel were, was nonetheless in a spiritual one.

Egypt's bondage was a type of that spiritual universal bondage. God had made a promise to Abram and his descendants to be with them and to deliver them. The Children of Israel's exodus out of there was a type of the spiritual universal deliverance. Christ's coming into the world was the means God used to redeem mankind from their inherited bondage and restored to a relationship with Him. (Acts 13:32-33). Everyone who chooses to receive Jesus Christ as Savior is not only delivered from the bondage of sin, but also given the "power to become sons of God" (John 1:12), as "sons of God" are inheritors of Canaan.

NOW WHAT?

While the Canaan in Abram's and his descendants' day was located in a particular geographic region of the world, Canaan for today's believers is not a specific geographic place. For believers today, Canaan is the starting point of a personal pilgrimage of faith in God–a journey that begins at the time of the "new birth" and ends at arrival in heaven. This means every "born again" believer today resides in the spiritual land of Canaan. It is a journey during which believers by their general conduct demonstrate their faith in God.

My Canaan journey literally started when I was eleven years old, when I witnessed firsthand a notable miracle: the restoring of my Uncle Wilbert's crushed foot.

The Public Works Department was in the process of bringing electricity to various parts of the island. At that time, most of the work was done by manual labor. The installation process involved three or four men manually hoisting huge wooden utility poles and placing them securely in the ground to carry the electrical wires. My Uncle Wilbert was one of the men hired to do the work.

Reportedly, while Uncle Wilbert and other of the workers were hoisting one of the poles, it accidentally slipped out of their hands and landed on Uncle Wilbert's foot. They immediately rushed him to the hospital. When the doctors examined his foot, they concluded that because the foot was severely crushed, major surgery or amputation of the foot was his only option.

Neither my mother nor I heard of the accident until my Aunt Florence (Uncle Wilbert's wife) came to tell us. We were both in shock as she shared with us the details of the accident and what the doctors were proposing. In spite of being shocked, I thought to myself, "there has to be something else that can be done for Uncle Wilbert besides performing surgery or taking off his foot." I knew there was nothing physically I could do to help him, but as I watched the increasing sadness on my mother's and my Aunt Florence's face and I listened to them rehash Uncle Wilbert's condition, I started thinking about John 1:12: *"as many as received Him, to them gave He power to become the sons of God, even to them that believe on His name."* I started repeating the verse as if I was just learning it. (Faith certainly "comes by hearing, and hearing by the word of God"; not just hearing the word of God being spoken, but also by personally speaking the word of God to yourself.) Moments later, I began sensing an overwhelming feeling of confidence. Then I said to myself, "because I received Jesus Christ as my Savior, I am a saved person. This means I am God's child; and because I am God's child, I am able to do something to help my Uncle Wilbert get well."

Admittedly there was so much about being saved that I did not know. For example, I did not know salvation was more than just a guarantee for getting to heaven when I die. I did not know receiving Jesus Christ as my Savior brings me into a relationship with God and makes me an heir of heaven's provisions. Provisions that include healing, protection, wisdom, along with the indwelling presence of the Holy Spirit, to comfort, teach, and guide every saved person.

Several weeks passed and Uncle Wilbert was still in the hospital, still unable to walk and still facing the possibility of major foot surgery or amputation.

In spite of my then limited knowledge and understanding of the benefits and privileges of being saved, I had a good amount of certainty God was bigger and stronger than everyone and everything. To Him, Uncle Wilbert's crushed foot was a small thing. In the days that followed proof of that certainty became a living reality to me.

One Saturday morning, I was doing one of my weekly chores, taking groceries to my maternal grandparents who were living six miles from where my mother and I lived. This meant each visit to them was a twelve-mile round-trip walk I often did by myself. For me though one of the advantages of walking twelve miles alone through wide-open green fields was I had lots of time and space to think. On that particular Saturday morning I was doing a lot of thinking. I was thinking especially about Uncle Wilbert's crushed foot and wondering what could I do to help him get well. Realistically, there didn't appear to be anything an eleven-year-old child could do to help a grown adult who was lying in a hospital bed with a crushed foot.

As I continued my trek through the open green fields, looking up at the beautiful cloudless skies, I suddenly felt a strong presence of assurance come upon me and I said to myself, "God is up in heaven and He knows about Uncle Wilbert's crushed foot."

After that, I began singing a song I had learned in church, "Just a Closer Walk with Thee", particularly the verse that says, *"Through this world of toils and snares, If I falter, Lord who cares? Who with me my burden shares? None but Thee, Dear Lord, none but Thee."* Right away, it was as though I was surrounded by an indescribable presence; a presence that moved me to verbally (in my own childish way) ask God to help Uncle Wilbert. With uncontrollable tears rolling down my face, I said out loudly, "Dear Lord, please heal my Uncle Wilbert's foot." That was the only time I remember specifically asking God to heal Uncle Wilbert's foot.

Within weeks after praying that prayer, one sunny Friday morning, while my mother and I were hanging clothes out to dry, to our amazement Uncle Wilbert came walking up the hill to my mother's house. He was walking without the use of a cane. Excitedly, we both dropped the clothes and ran toward Uncle Wilbert.

After lots of hugging, jumping up and down, and "thank you Jesus" from my mother, we all went inside the house and excitedly listened to Uncle Wilbert tell his story. While he was telling all the details about the accident and of his time in the hospital, I quietly and eagerly looked down to see the crushed foot. To my astonishment, the foot was completely normal. Then Uncle Wilbert (as if he knew I was examining his foot) shouted out, "Look at my foot now and there was no need for any surgery."

I am pretty sure there were others who prayed for the healing of Uncle Wilbert's foot. What was most amazing to me, and which subsequently became a landmark in the development of my faith in

God, was that as a saved eleven-year-old child, I prayed to God and He answered my prayer.

Following the healing of Uncle Wilbert's foot was my personal experience of God's healing power when He healed me of repeated severe attacks of tonsillitis. As a child it felt like whenever I got wet in the rain, my tonsils would swell up severely. That condition persisted until I was about twelve years old. One particular attack was so bad, my mother had to take me to the hospital emergency room, where, when the doctor examined my throat, he grimly told my mother that my tonsils needed to be taken out as soon as possible and we make the appointment right away for it to be done. The doctor left us in the room and went to his office to look at his calendar for a date to schedule the surgery. While we were waiting for him to return to the room I saw my mother (as it were) deliberately put her hand over her mouth and did not say a word. When the doctor returned and offered the available dates to do the surgery, to my surprise, and I believe to the doctor's as well, my mother looked directly at the doctor and quietly, but courageously said to him, "Doctor, I thank you for examining my daughter's throat, goodbye." She then took me by my hand and said, "come on Edna; we are going home," and we both walked out of the hospital.

On the way home neither of us said anything to each other, mostly because my throat was hurting so badly, it hurt even just to breathe. As soon as we got inside the house, my mother held me by my shoulders, looked at me straight in the eyes and said, "Child, I am going to pray for you and God is going to heal your tonsils." By this time, it was easy for me to believe that God could and would heal my tonsils; I had seen Him heal my Uncle Wilbert's foot. My mother then put both her hands on my throat and said, "Lord, in the name of Jesus I ask you to please heal Edna's tonsils, Amen." In a matter of hours, I started feeling better. To my recollection that was the last attack of tonsillitis I had until I became an adult in my late twenties.

In relation to *Canaan, Now What*, those childhood experiences have helped to form the launching pad from which I embarked on my personal journey of faith in God. They, along with the Bible stories, have helped to create the basis for my decision to trust God, believe

His word, and rely on Him for protection, provision, and direction in every area and in every stage of my life. In fact, as I got older, both physically and spiritually, I have come to realize the Bible stories, although written long ago, are exceedingly relevant to every time, to every season, and to every people; they are indeed *"written for our learning"* and *"that through them we might have hope."* Hope — not only an expectation of going to heaven, but the wherewithal to live confidently and victoriously in this present world (1 Cor. 10:1; Rom. 15:4).

In reality, for believers today, Canaan encompasses the entire world. Similar to the physical Canaan which, when the Children of Israel arrived in it, was still occupied by heathen nations, in the same way spiritual Canaan, where believers enter once they are delivered from the bondage of sin (when they receive Jesus Christ as Savior), is inhabited by people who seemingly do not know God, neither do they reverence Him. People who apparently are controlled and motivated by ungodly forces. Yet, like the heathens of the Children of Israel's day — they too are among those for whom Christ came to set free from the bondage of sin.

In addition to Canaan for today's believers, being a lifelong personal pilgrimage of faith in God, it is also what Heb. 4:9 refers to as *"a rest for the people of God."* It is a place where, in spite of the "evil that is in the world," believers are nevertheless kept from it. Basically, it is a place or position where believers rely totally on God and trust Him for their sustenance.

Just as God had provided the resources for those of the Children of Israel who entered the physical land of Canaan, resources which for the most part were physical. For example, the goodly houses, milk, honey. In the same way, He has today provided the resources for those whom He has delivered from the bondage of sin. The believer today has been given "all things that pertain to life and godliness" (2 Pet. 1:3). This means God's provision for a believer goes far beyond material substance. It extends to provisions of spiritual substance, such as the peace of God that controls, preserves, and sustains in times of adversity. It includes the wisdom of God to discern good from evil and to make right choices in every situation.

It includes the "ever present" presence of the Holy Spirit which is Christ Himself living in every believer enabling them "to become the sons of God," who consistently demonstrate the characteristics of God in their day-to-day living.

Essentially, Canaan has to do with how we live our lives on a daily basis. Since this entire world is today the believer's Canaan, it is here that there is both the privilege and the opportunity to not only serve God, but to also be the indisputable evidence of their miraculous deliverance from the bondage of sin to a life of victory over it.

Though Jesus Christ, through His death, burial, and resurrection has redeemed all of mankind; still there are people residing in this world alongside believers who have not received Him as their Savior. As a result they remain mentally, emotionally, and spiritually enslaved. Believers living among them are to be a radiating symbol of hope. They, by their irreproachable conduct in the home, in the marketplace, and in the community, are to demonstrate their liberation from the entanglement of sin by being examples of right and truth.

Overall, in this spiritual land of Canaan, believers are to be the living visible proof of the delivering, protecting, and providing power of God—a power that is available to all who choose to believe God, to trust Him, and to obey Him. It is my hope *Canaan, Now What?* will inspire many to be that witness.

www.ingramcontent.com/pod-product-compliance
Ingram Content Group UK Ltd.
Pitfield, Milton Keynes, MK11 3LW, UK
UKHW022218230426
12048UKWH00016BA/923